Sandy,
the California Sea Otter

Happy House

About Wise & Wide

- A systematic 6-level English reading program based on Lexile® measures
- Diverse and interesting topics chosen from the elementary curriculums of Korea and English speaking western countries
- Well-written books in various forms including fiction stories, descriptive texts, and classics retold
- The informative but original fiction stories grab your interest, leading to the easy and clear understanding of the educational content.
- Improve thinking skills with solid after-reading activities at all levels of the series.

Wise & Wide is a 6-level English reading program that consists of 60 books and each level is systematically divided by Lexile® measures. The Lexile® Framework for Reading is the most popular reading measuring system in American formal education curriculums and many English programs. Over 20 out of 50 states in the U.S. mark Lexile® measures directly on students' final report cards and over 300 well-known publishers adopt and use Lexile® measures.

Experience many kinds of readings written by professional writers from the U.S. and England. They used interesting topics that were carefully chosen after analyzing elementary curriculums from around the world including Korea, the U.S., England, and Australia among many others. Comprehensive after-reading activities including graphic organizers, speaking tasks, and After-reading Tests are ready for you.

Levels in the series and their corresponding Lexile® measures

Level	Lexile® measures	U.S. Grade
Level 1	Below 200L	Pre K - K
Level 2	190L - 400L	Lower Grade 1
Level 3	350L - 530L	Upper Grade 1
Level 4	420L - 650L	Grade 2
Level 5	520L - 940L	Grade 3 - 4
Level 6	830L - 1070L	Grade 5 - 6

* Smart Readers: Wise & Wide level 1 is applicable to the preschool level in the U.S.

* The source of the relationship between Lexile® measures and U.S. school grades: CCSS(Common Core State Standards) FOR ENGLISH LANGUAGE ARTS, APPENDIX A (2012, which is used by 45 states in the U.S.)

Topic List

	Level 1	Level 2	Level 3	Level 4	Level 5	Level 6
Book 1	Science>Biology: The hibernation of animals Story	Science>Biology: Living and nonliving things Story	Science>Biology> Animals & the Environment: Sea otters Story	Environment> Living with nature: The diver & the persimmon tree Story	Science>Biology> Animal: Amazing animals of the Amazon Story	Science>Biology: Germs, transmitted diseases Story
Book 2	Literature> World classics: Aesop's fables Story	Literature> Traditional fairy tale: Old tales about stones Story	Social Studies> Economy: To run a business to make and save money Story	Science>Biology> Plants: Photosynthesis Story	Science>Earth science: Earth's layers, earthquakes, volcanoes, and earth's atmosphere Report	Mathematics> Sequence: The golden ratio & the Fibonacci sequence Story
Book 3	Science>Physics: How shadows are formed Story	Literature> World classics: Peter Pan Story	Science>Scientific technology: Nanobots Story	Literature>Myths: World's creation stories Story	Literature> Legend: The story of King Arthur Story	Literature>Myths: Constellation myths Story
Book 4	Literature> Traditional literature: The Talmud Story	Science>Biology> Animal: Polar bears Story	Science>Biology> Animal: Mountain gorillas Story	Social Studies> Cultural anthropology: Amazing ancient cultures of the world Story	Science> Earth science: Clouds and weather Story	Literature> Human & animals: The friendship between a girl and a horse Story
Book 5	Social Studies> Ethics: Rules in daily life Story	Science>Biology: The five senses Report	Social Studies> Cultural anthropology: Astonishing festivals Report	Art>Music: Stories from two operas Story	Social Studies> World culture & history: The Renaissance Story	Sports> Board sports: Surfing & snowboarding Story
Book 6	Social Studies> World geography & travel: Tourist attractions around the world Story	Science>Biology> Animal: Dinosaurs Story	Science> Astronomy: The solar system Story	Social Studies> People: Three great people who overcame hardships Story	Science>Scientific technology: The wonderful world of robots Report	Art>Music: Composers of the Romantic Era Report
Book 7	Science> Space science: The life of astronauts Report	Social Studies> Cultural anthropology: Mythological monsters from around the world Report	Mathematics> Elementary mathematics: Numbers, measurement, shapes and data Report	Science & Social Studies> Technology & culture: Inventions from around the world Report	Art>Works of art: Famous paintings Report	Social Studies> Human & animals: Animals in action for human Report
Book 8	Social Studies> Cultural anthropology: Various living cultures of the world Story	Art>Music: Instruments in the orchestra Story	Social Studies> Life safety: Learning and using outdoor survival skills Story	Social Studies> History: The California Gold Rush Report	Social Studies & Science> Psychology: Psychology in everyday life Story	Literature> World classics: The Merchant of Venice Story
Book 9	Social Studies> Jobs: Interviews about jobs Report	Science>Scientific technology: Developments in technology in different times Story	Social Studies> Politics>Election: Running for 3rd grade class president Story	Literature> World classics: Stories of Sherlock Holmes Story	Literature> World classics: Adrift in the Pacific Story	Social Studies> History & People: Great world leaders in history Report
Book 10	Literature>Traditional fairy tale: Eastern and Western folk tales on the same theme Story	Sports>Winter sports: Various aspects of some Winter Olympic sports Report	Literature> World classics: Short stories by O. Henry Story	Sports> Ball games: Various aspects of popular ball games Report	Social Studies> History: Famous events that changed world history Report	Art & Social Studies> Art: Stories about the creation, distribution, and preservation of paintings Report

How to Use This Book

•Before Reading

You can easily find the topic and what kind of story you are about to read.

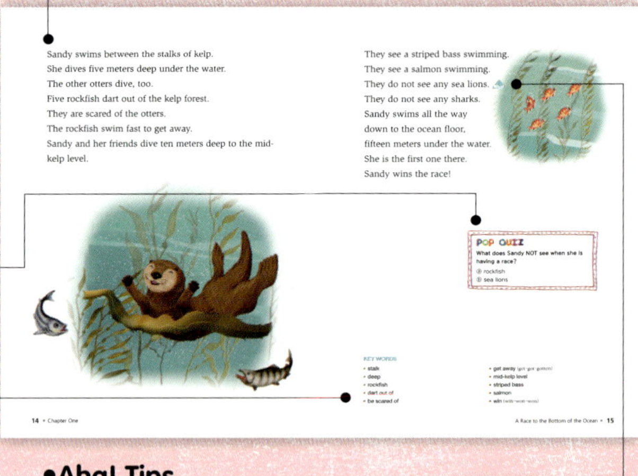

•The text

All the stories were written by professional writers from the U.S. and England, so you will read authentic and appropriate English sentences and expressions in every book in the series.

•Pop Quiz

Check out right away if you understand what you have just read by solving a pop quiz that checks your comprehension.

•Key Words

The key words and expressions on each page are listed for you to easily study them.

•Aha! Tips

Download free Korean explanations at *www.ihappyhouse.co.kr* for all of the sentences marked with "Aha!". These explain cultural, scientific, and economic knowledge or they deal with aspects of English such as grammatical structures or idiomatic expressions. There are lots of "Aha! Tips" to help you understand the text.

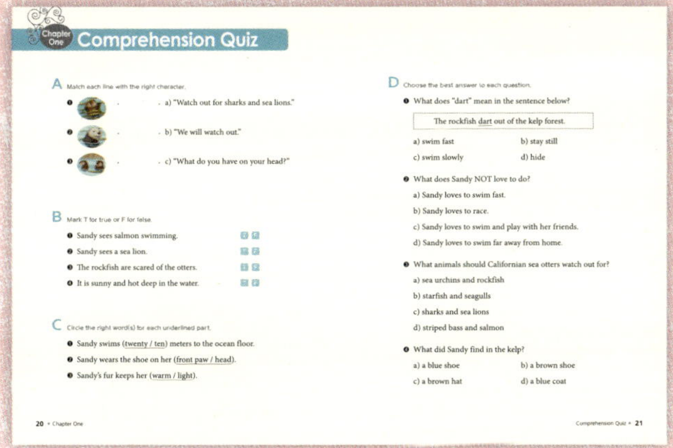

•Comprehension Quiz

After reading one chapter, solve various questions to find out if you fully understand the content.

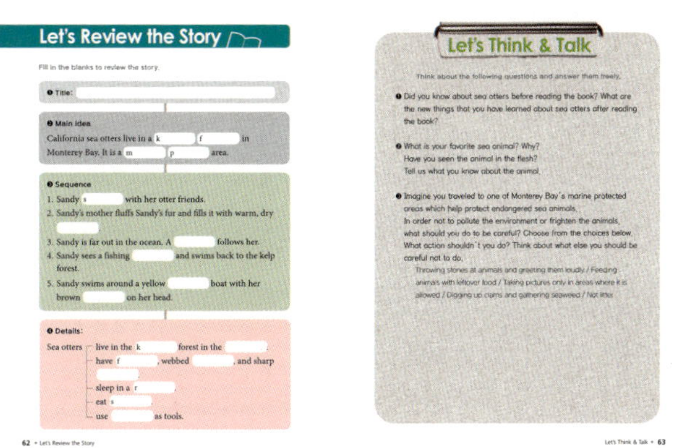

•Let's Review the Story /
•Let's Think & Talk

Fill in the blanks in the organizer to summarize the whole story. Express your own thinking and feelings about the story by answering the questions. You can build up logic and reasoning skills for your essay examinations in the future.

Appendix

Audio CD
In the CD audio book form, the texts are read vividly by American professional voice actors.

After-reading Test
Solve an additionally provided After-reading Test for each book.

The Korean translation, Answer Keys, a Word Quiz, a Word List, and Aha! Tips for each book
You can download them for free at *www.ihappyhouse.co.kr*

Before Reading

Sandy, the California Sea Otter

Level 3-1,
Lexile® 480L

•Science 〉 Biology 〉 Animals & the Environment
•Story

Do you know what a sea otter is?

A sea otter is called '해달' in Korean. The main character in the animation *Bono Bono* is a sea otter. Sea otters usually live in groups in the sea and eat clams, sea urchins, abalones, and other crustaceans. They can swim fast thanks to their hind legs that look like paddles. They are also clever enough to use tools. They find clams, put them on their bellies, break the shells using stones and then they take out the delicious clam meat. Lying face upwards and floating on the sea, they look super cute and happy when they eat clams that they put on their belly. They are so neat that they clean their whiskers and face using their paws and spin their body in the water to wash away food scraps after eating.

But the clever and cute sea otters are endangered now and protected by people. Hunters have hunted them down for a long time because their fur is shiny and lovely enough to be used to make the highest quality of fur coats.

A place where animals live happily can also be a place where people live happily, can't it? Please consider animals as well as humans as part of nature as both of them are equally precious.

Summary

In the book, you will meet a young sea otter, Sandy which lives in the Gulf of California. A sea otter's amazing life will spread before your eyes when you read about Sandy's daily life and adventures.

Sandy is a young sea otter living in Monterey Bay in California. Sandy is second to none in swimming and specially likes fresh sea urchins. Sandy's everyday life is fun and peaceful. Sandy competes with his friends in swimming, preys on fresh and delicious sea urchins and mussels with his mom and takes a nap while floating on the sea.

One day, Sandy was swimming alone after napping. Being engrossed in watching the sunlight shining like jewelry on the sea, Sandy swam too far away from his home. There was no one but Sandy out in that part of the vast sea. Oh my, suddenly, there was a huge black shadow!

Contents

Sandy, the California Sea Otter

Sandy,
the California Sea Otter

Chapter One

A Race to the Bottom of the Ocean

Sandy, a California sea otter, loves to splash and play. *Aha!*

She is swimming in a kelp forest in the ocean waters
of Monterey Bay. *Aha!*

Some of Sandy's friends say, "Do you want to have a
race?"

Sandy loves to race. She can swim fast.

Sandy's webbed feet help her swim fast.

She can dive deep in the cold water.

Her fur keeps her warm.

The otter pups line up in the water.

They all keep their heads above the water.

Sandy's mother says, "Watch out for sharks and sea
lions.

Sometimes sharks and sea lions bite California sea
otters."

Sandy tells her mother, "We will
stay in the kelp forest.
We will watch out."

▲ a sea otter lying in the kelp fronds

- race
- bottom of the ocean
- sea otter
- splash
- swim (swim-swam-swum)
- kelp forest
- ocean water

- Monterey Bay
- love to + *Verb*
- webbed
- dive
- deep
- fur
- keep (keep-kept-kept)

- pup
- line up
- watch out
- shark
- sea lion
- bite
- stay

The otter pups are all ready to race.

One otter friend says, "Ready. Set. Go!"

They all start to swim.

Sandy dives all the way to the ocean floor.

She closes her ear flaps to keep the water out of her ears.

She closes her nostrils to hold her breath.

She kicks with her back legs and tail.

She holds her front paws to her chest.

Sandy dives under the canopy of the kelp forest.

The big green fronds look like leaves in the water.

The sun shines on the kelp forest, and the fronds make shade.

The waves of the ocean make the kelp sway in the water.

It looks like a tree in the wind.

KEY WORDS

- be ready to
- Ready. Set. Go!
- all the way
- ocean floor
- ear flap
- nostril
- hold one's breath
  (hold-held-held)
- kick
- tail
- hold
- front paw
- chest
- canopy
- frond
- shine (shine-shone-shone)
- make shade
  (make-made-made)
- wave
- sway
- look like

Sandy swims between the stalks of kelp.

She dives five meters deep under the water.

The other otters dive, too.

Five rockfish dart out of the kelp forest.

They are scared of the otters.

The rockfish swim fast to get away.

Sandy and her friends dive ten meters deep to the mid-kelp level.

They see a striped bass swimming.

They see a salmon swimming.

They do not see any sea lions. 

They do not see any sharks.

Sandy swims all the way

down to the ocean floor,

fifteen meters under the water.

She is the first one there.

Sandy wins the race!

POP QUIZ

What does Sandy NOT see when she is having a race?

ⓐ rockfish
ⓑ sea lions

KEY WORDS

- stalk
- deep
- rockfish
- dart out of
- be scared of

- get away (get-got-gotten)
- mid-kelp level
- striped bass
- salmon
- win (win-won-won)

It is very shady this deep in the water.

Sandy swims with her otter friends.

They play in the kelp fronds.

She sees some red kelp crabs and purple sea urchins.

They are in the holdfast of the kelp forest. 

The holdfast is where the kelp attaches to the rocks on

the seafloor.

▲ holdfast of the kelp

POP QUIZ

Choose the right words for the underlined part.

Some red kelp crabs are (ⓐ under the canopy / ⓑ in the holdfast) of the kelp forest.

- shady
- kelp crab
- purple
- sea urchin
- holdfast
- attach

- seafloor (= seabed)
- something else
- clam
- mussel
- take a closer look

Sandy sees something else in the kelp holdfast.

It is not a red kelp crab.

It is not a purple sea urchin.

It is not a clam or a mussel.

What is it?

She swims over to take a closer look. Aha!

It is a brown shoe!

Sandy has seen fishermen wearing shoes on their feet. Aha!

Sandy wants to wear it.

But Sandy doesn't have any feet.

She puts the shoe on her head. Aha!

She wears it like a hat.

KEY WORDS

- brown
- fishermen
- wear (wear-wore-worn)
- feet
- put on
- like
- up
- surface
- funny
- have a good time

POP QUIZ

What did Sandy find at the bottom of the ocean?

→ a ________ ________

She swims up from the bottom of the ocean.

She swims up to the mid-kelp level.

She swims up to the canopy.

She swims up to the surface of the water.

Her friends laugh and say, "What do you have on your head, Sandy?"

Sandy swims around with the shoe on her head.

She thinks it is funny.

Her friends think it is funny, too.

Sandy is having a good time.

Comprehension Quiz

A Match each line with the right character.

❶  · · a) "Watch out for sharks and sea lions."

❷  · · b) "We will watch out."

❸ · · c) "What do you have on your head?"

B Mark T for true or F for false.

❶ Sandy sees salmon swimming.   T F

❷ Sandy sees a sea lion.   T F

❸ The rockfish are scared of the otters.   T F

❹ It is sunny and hot deep in the water.   T F

C Circle the right word(s) for each underlined part.

❶ Sandy swims (twenty / ten) meters to the ocean floor.

❷ Sandy wears the shoe on her (front paw / head).

❸ Sandy's fur keeps her (warm / light).

❶ What does "dart" mean in the sentence below?

> The rockfish <u>dart</u> out of the kelp forest.

a) swim fast   b) stay still

c) swim slowly   d) hide

❷ What does Sandy NOT love to do?

a) Sandy loves to swim fast.

b) Sandy loves to race.

c) Sandy loves to swim and play with her friends.

d) Sandy loves to swim far away from home.

❸ What animals should Californian sea otters watch out for?

a) sea urchins and rockfish

b) starfish and seagulls

c) sharks and sea lions

d) striped bass and salmon

❹ What did Sandy find in the kelp?

a) a blue shoe   b) a brown shoe

c) a brown hat   d) a blue coat

Chapter Two

Hunting in the Kelp Forest

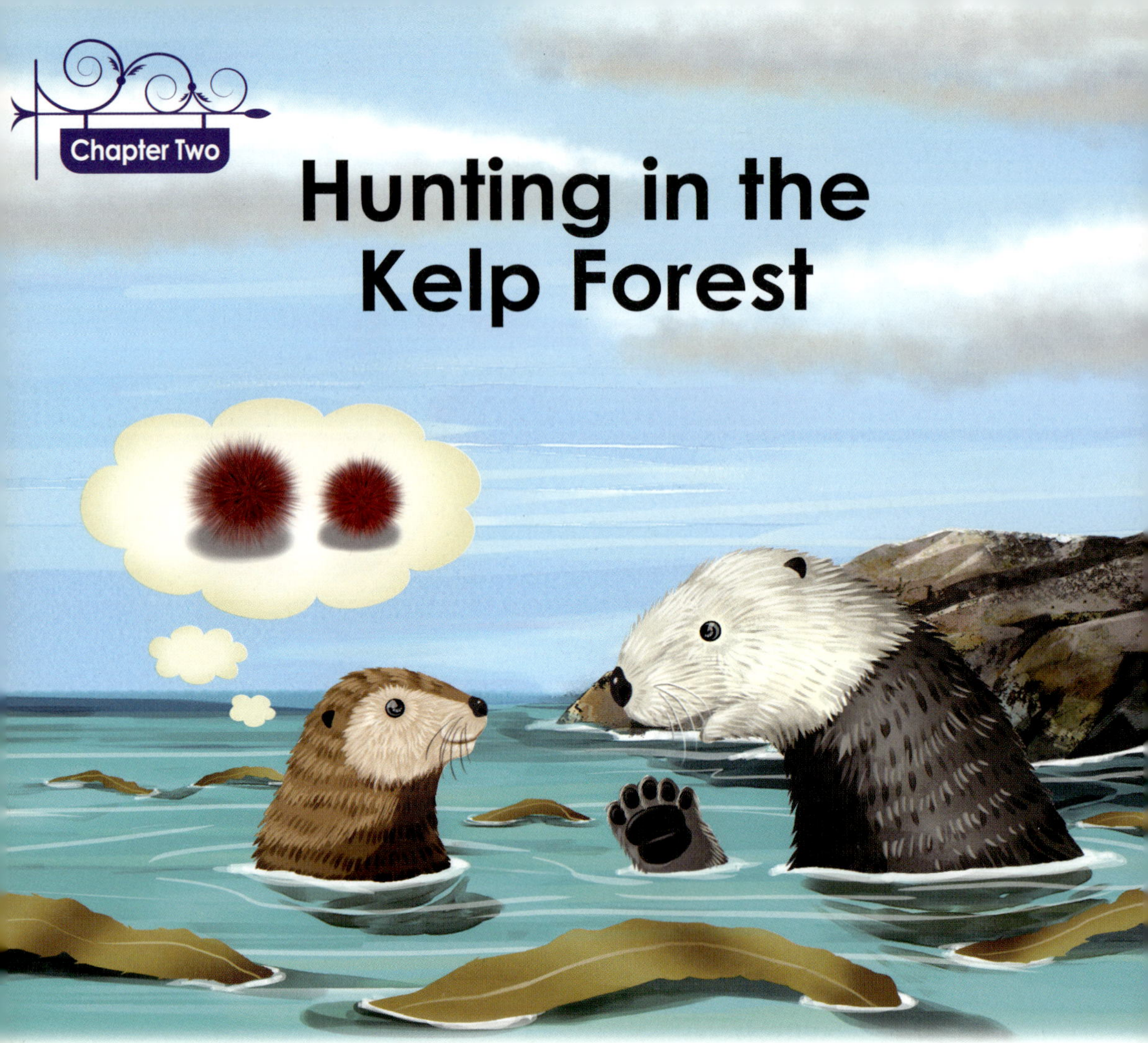

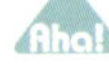

Sandy's mother whistles.

Whistling is how she calls Sandy. Aha!

"Come and get lunch!"

The other otter mothers whistle to their otter pups.

It is lunchtime for all of them.

All of the swimming and diving has made Sandy hungry.

"Will we have kelp crabs for lunch, Mom?" Sandy asks.

"Perhaps," her mother says.

"May we have sea urchins for lunch?

They taste so good!" Sandy says.

"We may," her mother says.

"How about some nice, juicy sea snails?" Aha!

"All of those can be our lunch," her mother says.

"Get ready to dive down deep, my little pup."

POP QUIZ

How does a sea otter mother call her pups?

ⓐ by whistling
ⓑ by waving her front paws

KEY WORDS

- hunt
- whistle
- call
- lunchtime
- may
- taste
- juicy
- sea snail

Sandy takes a big breath of air.

She fills her big lungs.

She follows her mother underwater.

They see a jewel top snail.

It is eating a kelp frond in the mid-kelp level. 

"Hi, Jewel!" Sandy says as she swims past.

Sandy and her mother swim all the way to the ocean
floor.

Sandy's mother grabs a spiny sea urchin with her claw
and a rock with her other claw.

She puts the sea urchin under her arm.

She uses the sharp rock to knock a mussel off the
seafloor.

She puts the mussel under her arm with the sea urchin.

Sandy does the same thing.

KEY WORDS

- take a big breath of air
- fill
- lung
- underwater
- jewel
- jewel top snail
- snail
- past
- grab
- spiny
- claw
- put (put-put-put)
- arm
- sharp
- knock
- do the same thing

They swim up to the surface of the water.

Sandy's mother rolls onto her back.

Sandy does the same thing.

Sandy and her mother bite open the sea urchins with
their sharp front teeth.

They lick the tasty sea urchin meat.

"Yum, yum!" Sandy says.

"Sea urchins are my favorite meal."

"That is good to hear," Sandy's mother says.

"Sea urchins eat the kelp in the ocean.

We need to eat sea urchins so that they do not destroy
our home."

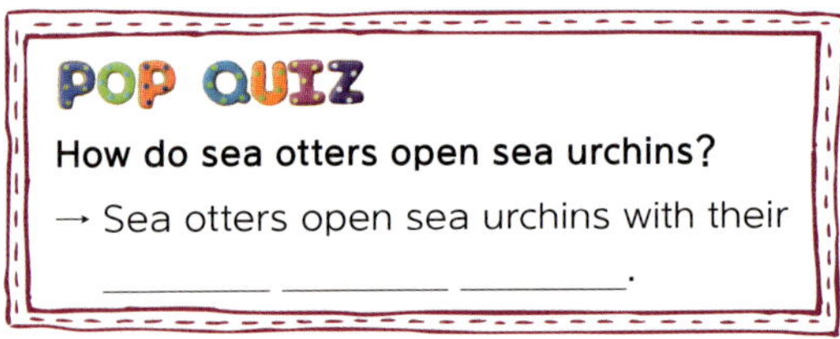

POP QUIZ

How do sea otters open sea urchins?

→ Sea otters open sea urchins with their
______________ ______________ ______________.

KEY WORDS

- roll onto one's back
- teeth
- lick
- tasty
- yum
- favorite
- meal

- destroy
- all day
- take out (take-took-taken)
- float on one's back
- pull
- twist

"I want to eat more sea urchins," Sandy says.

She licks her lips. She licks her paws.

"I can eat sea urchins all day."

"First, we must eat our mussels," her mother says.

Sandy takes the mussel out from under her arm.

She floats on her back and uses her claws to try to open the shell.

But the shell does not open.

She pulls harder and twists it.

The shell still does not open.

"Watch me," Sandy's mother says.
She puts the rock on her stomach.
She hits the mussel on the rock. 
The shell breaks open!
Sandy's mother eats the juicy mussel.
Sandy thinks that is a good idea.

KEY WORDS

- **hit** (hit-hit-hit)
- **break open**
- **pull out**
- **catch** (catch-caught-caught)
- **dig** (dig-dug-dug)

She takes out her rock and hits her mussel on it.

It does not open. Sandy hits it again.

It still does not open.

She hits it one more time, and this time the shell opens!

She uses her claw to pull out the mussel and eats the tasty meat.

Sandy and her mother dive for food many more times.

Sandy's mother catches a rockfish with her claws.

Sandy's mother digs in the ocean bottom.

She gets a clam.

She opens the clam by hitting it on a rock.

They eat snails, kelp crabs, sea urchins, and rockfish.

When they finish eating, Sandy is full and sleepy.

"You must clean yourself before you take a nap,"
Sandy's mother tells her.

Sandy spins around and around in the water.

Spinning in the water is fun, and it cleans the food off
her thick fur.

She licks all the food off her paws and claws.

She rubs her face to clean her long, brown whiskers.

When she is old, her
face and whiskers
will turn white
like her mother's.
Sandy's mother
says, "Come and
lie on my stomach, little
pup."
Sandy's mother floats on her back in the water.
Sandy climbs on her mother's stomach.

KEY WORDS

- finish
- full
- sleepy
- clean off
- take a nap

- spin
- thick
- lick off
- rub
- whisker

- turn
- lie (lie-lay-lain)
- stomach
- climb

Sandy's mother picks up the fur on her pup and blows on it.

She brushes Sandy's fur. She blows on Sandy's fur.

This fluffs Sandy's fur and fills it with warm, dry air.

When Sandy's mother finishes fluffing Sandy's fur, it is so full of warm air that she floats.

She cannot dive now. Her fur is too fluffy.

She rolls in the kelp fronds.

The kelp fronds will be her bed.

Then, she holds paws with her mother and yawns.

KEY WORDS

- pick up
- blow
  (blow-blew-blown)
- brush
- fluff
- be full of
- fluffy
- yawn
- raft
- coo
- soft
- rock

All the other otters lie in the kelp fronds and hold paws.

This keeps them together in a raft while they sleep.

"Sweet dreams, little pup," Sandy's mother tells her.

She coos to her.

The water is cold.

The sun is warm.

The waves are soft.

The soft ocean waves rock the raft of otters to sleep.

Chapter Two — Comprehension Quiz

A Mark T for true or F for false.

❶ Sandy and her mother float on their stomachs.　T　F

❷ Sandy's mother finds a clam at the ocean bottom.　T　F

❸ Sandy's mother tells her to lie down on her stomach.　T　F

❹ Sandy's mother fluffs Sandy's fur by blowing on it.　T　F

B Circle the right word(s) for each underlined part.

❶ Sea otter mothers call to their pups by (whistling / singing).

❷ The jewel top snail is eating a (kelp frond / sea urchin).

❸ When Sandy is old, her face and whiskers will turn (brown / white) like her mother's.

❹ Sandy uses her (claw / teeth) to pull out the mussel meat.

❺ (Ocean waves / Sandy's mother) rock(s) the otters to sleep.

❶ What is NOT one of Sandy's favorite foods?

a) striped bass

b) kelp crabs

c) sea urchins

d) juicy sea snails

❷ What did Sandy's mother grab at the ocean floor?

a) a spiny sea urchin and a rock

b) a brown shoe

c) a piece of kelp

d) a starfish

❸ How do Sandy and her mother open the sea urchins?

a) with rocks

b) with their webbed feet

c) with their sharp front teeth

d) by squeezing the sea urchins

❹ How does Sandy's mother catch a rockfish?

a) She catches it in a net.

b) She catches it with her claws.

c) She catches it in her mouth.

d) She traps it in the kelp.

Chased by a Shark

When Sandy wakes up, the sun is still shining.

She wants to play.

She wants to swim, dive, and race.

All her friends are still asleep.

Should she wait for them to wake up?

Sandy knows she should wait,

but she wants to play now.

She wants to play with her

brown shoe.

She looks for her shoe in the kelp.

She cannot find it.

Where is her shoe?

Sandy swims around the kelp and looks for her shoe.

She swims far out to the edge of the kelp forest.

Sandy has never been this far out before. 

The sun sparkles on the ocean water.

It looks pretty. It looks like jewels sparkling on the water.

POP QUIZ

What does Sandy want to do when she wakes up? (Unscramble the letters to find the answer.)

→ She wants to <u>ylpa</u>.

KEY WORDS

- **wake up** (wake-woke-woken)
- **asleep**
- **should**
- **wait**
- **look for**
- **cannot**
- **far**
- **the edge of**
- **have never bee**
- **sparkle**
- **look pretty**

Sandy wants to see what the deep ocean looks like. 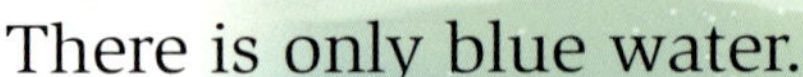
She dives underwater.
The sun shines through the water and sparkles on tiny
bubbles of air.
Sandy looks far out into the sea.
There is only blue water.

KEY WORDS

- tiny
- bubble
- follow
- turn to the left
- school
- have fun
- swim away

Sandy sees some fish swimming together in a school.

She follows them, and they turn to the left.

She follows them, and they turn to the right.

Sandy follows the school of fish.

They swim down, and they swim up.

Sandy swims down and swims up, too.

She is having fun.

Then, the fish swim away.

Sandy is all alone.

She does not see the kelp forest anymore.

She sees the blue ocean water.

She turns around, and all she sees is the blue ocean water. **Aha!**

She looks down.

She cannot see the bottom of the ocean.

She swims to the surface and looks.

She is very far away from land.

She is very far away from her kelp forest.

Sandy feels lonely.

Sandy feels scared.

She has never been alone before.

She has never been this far out in the ocean before.

She starts to swim back to the kelp forest.

She pushes hard with her back paws and her tail.

Sandy is swimming fast.

She is swimming almost nine kilometers an hour.

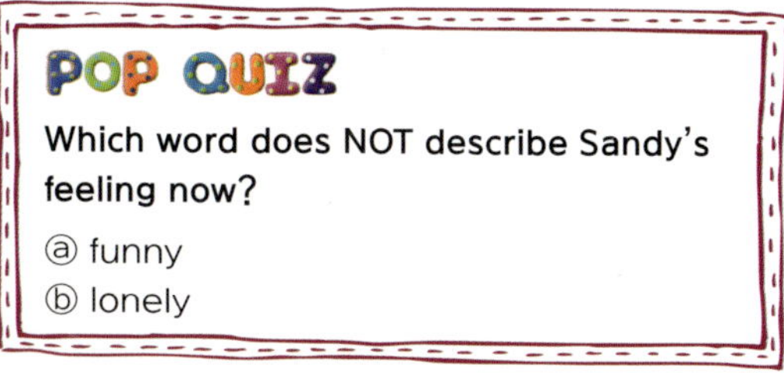

KEY WORDS

- all alone
- turn around
- look down
- far away

- feel lonely/scared
- start to + *Verb*
- push hard
- nine kilometers an hour

Sandy feels the water move under her.

She thinks it is a wave.

But it is not smooth like a wave.

She feels something move past her very fast.

Something big is swimming below her in the ocean.

She looks down and sees a shadow.

The shadow goes away and comes back.

It gets bigger.

KEY WORDS

- move
- below
- go away (go-went-gone)

- come back (come-came-come)
- bigger
- pump

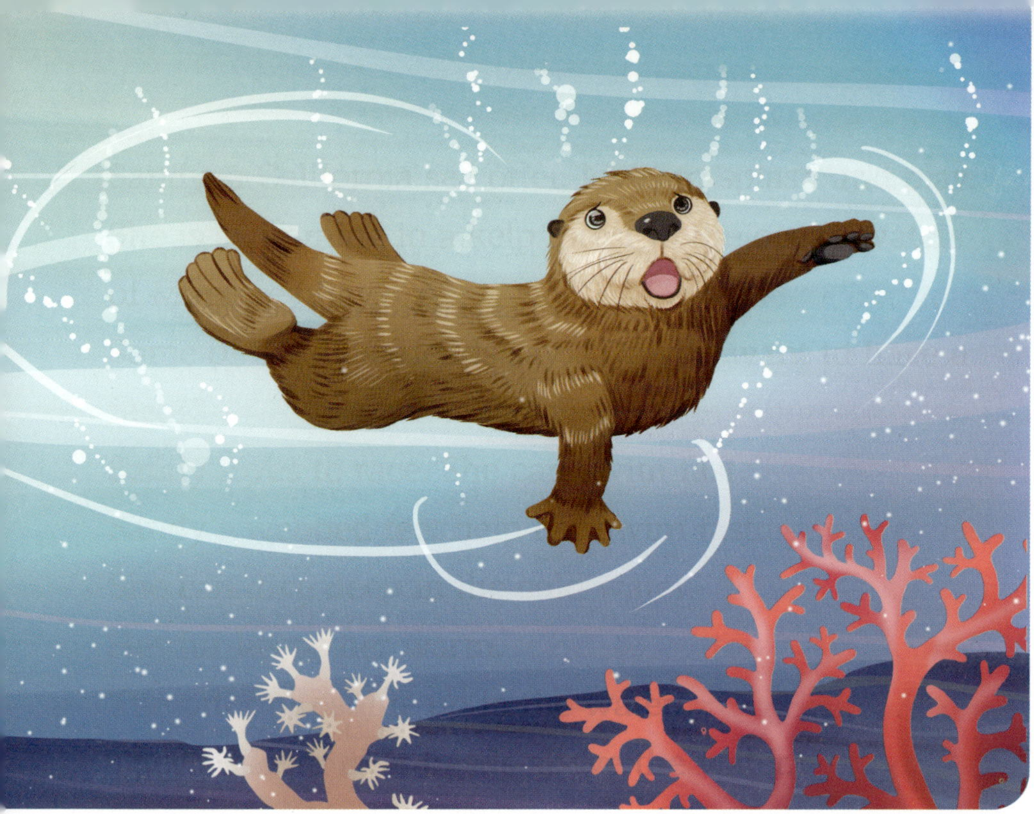

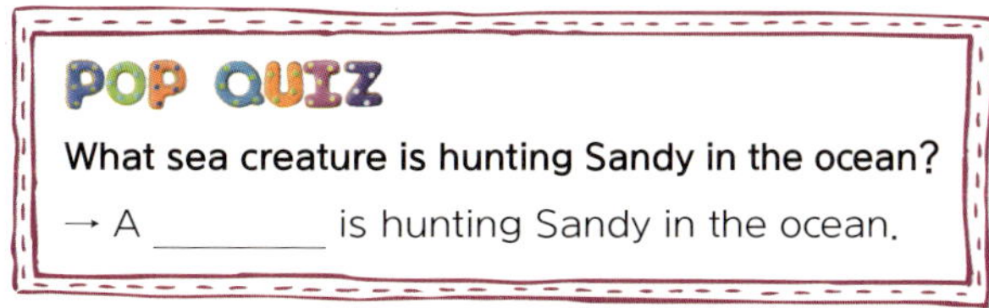

The shadow is a shark!

Her mother told her to watch out for sharks and sea lions.

Perhaps the shark wants to eat Sandy!

Sandy's heart pumps hard.

She swims fast.

Her webbed feet help her swim fast.

But the shark swims fast, too.

Sandy turns to the left.

The shark follows her.

Its mouth is open.

Its teeth are sharp.

Sandy turns to the right.

The shark follows her.

The shark is close.

Sandy dives down.

The shark dives down.

Sandy swims up.

The shark follows right on her tail.

Sandy swims as fast as she can. 

She needs to get back to the kelp forest.

Will she get away from the shark?

▲ one of the fastest fish in the ocean,
the Pacific sailfish

KEY WORDS

- as fast as one can
- get back to
- get away from

She hears a sound.

Thrum, thrum, thrum.

It is a motor. It is the motor on a fishing boat.

The shark hears the motor, too.

Thrum, thrum, thrum.

The fishing boat is coming closer.

The shark looks at Sandy.

Sandy keeps swimming.

The shark looks at the fishing boat.

Thrum, thrum, thrum.

The shark looks at Sandy one more time.

Then, it turns and swims away.

Sharks do not like fishing boats.

POP QUIZ

What does the shark do when it sees the fishing boat?

→ When the shark sees the fishing boat, it turns and __________ __________.

KEY WORDS

- thrum
- fishing boat
- keep + *Verb*-ing
- tired

- hide (hide-hid-hidden)
- pull
- net
- pass

Sandy is tired from swimming so fast.

She stops and hides in the water.

Only her nose and eyes are out of the water.

The motor on the fishing boat thrums.

She looks at the boat.

She sees the fisherman on the boat pulling a net.

She hears the motor.

Thrum, thrum, thrum.

The boat passes by her in the ocean.

Sandy hears her mother call her.

Her mother whistles.

Her mother is looking for her.

Sandy whistles to her mother.

Sandy hears her mother whistle louder.

Sandy swims back to the kelp forest.

Sandy's mother says, "Little pup, why did you swim so far away?"

Sandy cries, "I wanted to find my brown shoe.

Then, the ocean sparkled so pretty, and I swam far away."

Sandy hugs her mother and climbs onto her stomach.

Sandy's mother holds her pup with her paws.

She coos to tell Sandy she is safe.

KEY WORDS

- louder
- cry
- hug
- safe

Comprehension Quiz

A Mark T for true or F for false.

❶ Sandy follows the school of fish.　　T　F

❷ Sandy is all alone because the other otters swam away.　　T　F

❸ Sandy can still see the kelp forest when she is far out in the ocean.　　T　F

❹ Sandy likes to be alone in the ocean.　　T　F

B Write the right answer to each question.

❶ What does Sandy want to find when she swims far away from the kelp forest?

→ Her ________________ ________________.

❷ What looks like jewels sparkling on the water?

→ The ________________.

❸ What does Sandy climb onto?

→ Her mother's ________________.

 Choose the best answer to each question.

❶ What makes the sound Sandy hears when she swims away from the shark?

a) the motor on a fishing boat

b) someone beating on a drum

c) the waves on the shore

d) a whale tail splashing on the water

❷ Why does the shark swim away?

a) It is tired of playing chase.

b) It wants to go home.

c) It does not like fishing boats.

d) It finds another sea otter to chase.

❸ Which parts of Sandy's body are out of the water when she hides?

a) her stomach and paws

b) her tail and legs

c) her nose and eyes

d) her entire head

❹ How does Sandy's mother tell her she is safe?

a) She coos.   b) She hums.

c) She sings.   d) She whistles.

Protecting the Sea Otters

Later, Sandy's mother tells her, "You must never again swim away from the kelp forest."

Sandy promises to stay in the kelp.

Sandy's mother says, "The kelp forest is a marine protected area."

"What does that mean?" Sandy asks.

"It means we cannot be hunted here. We are safe to live here."

"I want to be safe," Sandy says.

"I want to play with my friends, swim, and dive."

POP QUIZ

In the story, why did hunters kill sea otters?

→ Hunters killed sea otters because they wanted the otters' __________ to make __________ .

KEY WORDS

- promise
- marine protected area
- mean (mean-meant-meant)
- coat

- gone
- endangered
- be protected

Sandy's mother tells her a story.

"A long time ago, hunters killed sea otters.

They wanted our soft fur."

"Why did they want our fur?" Sandy asks.

"They made coats out of our fur.

They hunted sea otters until we were almost all gone."

"That is sad," Sandy says.

"Yes, it is. Hunters even killed your grandparents."

Sandy wants to cry. "Will hunters kill us?"

"No, little pup." Sandy's mother fluffs her fur.

"Now, endangered sea otters are protected."

"I'm glad we're protected," Sandy rubs her face with her paws.

"You may play, swim, and dive in the marine protected area," her mother says.

"But never go into the deep ocean alone."

"I will stay in the kelp forest from now on," Sandy says.

Her mother coos and holds her paw.

Sandy feels safe.

"Are you hungry?" her mother asks.

Sandy is very hungry after all that swimming.

"Yes. I'm going to dive for more food."

She dives down to the holdfast to get a purple sea urchin.

When Sandy is underwater, she sees the brown shoe.

"I must have dropped my shoe!" Sandy thinks.

She puts the sea urchin in the shoe.

She puts the shoe on her head.

She swims to the surface.

She rolls up in a kelp frond.

She takes the shoe off her head.

She takes out the sea urchin.

She floats on her back.

Sandy bites open the sea urchin and licks out the meat.

"Yum, yum!"

Some people in a yellow rubber boat are floating nearby.

They have special glasses to look at the sea otters.

The people all wear hats.

Sandy wants to wear a hat like the people in the yellow rubber boat.

She rolls in the water to get clean.

She puts the shoe on her head.

She swims around the boat.

A woman takes a picture of Sandy with her camera.

"She is so cute," the woman says.

"She is so funny!" A boy laughs.

The boy is wearing a hat that looks like a jewel top snail.

Sandy thinks the boy is funny.

KEY WORDS

- rubber
- nearby
- special glasses

- around
- take a picture
- cute

Sandy swims around them in the water with the shoe
on her head.

She dives under the boat.

She pops up behind the boat.

The people laugh.

Sandy likes to have fun.

She likes living in the kelp forest.

Sandy is happy there are people who protect the sea
otters. **Aha!**

The sun is going down now.

The people in the yellow rubber boat go back to the land.

Sandy goes back to her friends and mother.

She rolls up in the kelp to take another nap.

When she wakes up, she will dive for more sea urchins.

Sandy loves the life of a California sea otter.

KEY WORDS

- pop up
- behind
- go down

- go back
- another

Chapter Four

Comprehension Quiz

A Mark T for true or F for false.

❶ Hunters killed Sandy's brother and sister.　　T　F

❷ Endangered sea otters are not protected.　　T　F

❸ Sandy dives to the holdfast to get a purple sea urchin.　　T　F

❹ Sandy put the purple sea urchin in the brown shoe.　　T　F

❺ The people in the yellow boat want to hunt the otters.　　T　F

B Choose the right word for each blank.

❶ The boy's hat looks like a jewel top ____________.
(rockfish / mussel / snail)

❷ Sandy thinks the boy is ____________. (sad / loud / funny)

❸ Sandy dives under the ____________. (boat / motor / shark)

❹ At the end of the story, the people in the yellow rubber boat go
back to the ____________. (house / ocean / land)

 Choose the best answer to each question.

❶ What does Sandy's mother tell her?

a) Never swim away from the kelp forest.

b) Come home when it gets dark.

c) Stay away from the kelp mid-level.

d) Don't swim too fast.

❷ What is a marine protected area?

a) a place where soldiers work

b) a place where endangered sea animals are safe to live

c) a place where fishermen live

d) a place where no sharks may swim

❸ Why did the hunters want the sea otters' fur?

a) to make soft beds

b) to make shoes

c) to make coats

d) to make rugs

Let's Review the Story

Fill in the blanks to review the story.

❶ Title: ________________________________

❷ Main idea

California sea otters live in a k_________ f_________ in Monterey Bay. It is a m_________ p_________ area.

❸ Sequence

1. Sandy s_________ with her otter friends.
2. Sandy's mother fluffs Sandy's fur and fills it with warm, dry _________.
3. Sandy is far out in the ocean. A _________ follows her.
4. Sandy sees a fishing _________ and swims back to the kelp forest.
5. Sandy swims around a yellow _________ boat with her brown _________ on her head.

❹ Details:

Sea otters
- live in the k_________ forest in the _________.
- have f_________, webbed _________, and sharp _________.
- sleep in a r_________.
- eat s_________.
- use _________ as tools.

Let's Think & Talk

Think about the following questions and answer them freely.

❶ Did you know about sea otters before reading the book? What are the new things that you have learned about sea otters after reading the book?

❷ What is your favorite sea animal? Why?
Have you seen the animal in the flesh?
Tell us what you know about the animal.

❸ Imagine you traveled to one of Monterey Bay's marine protected areas which help protect endangered sea animals.
In order not to pollute the environment or frighten the animals, what should you do to be careful? Choose from the choices below. What action shouldn't you do? Think about what else you should be careful not to do.

> Throwing stones at animals and greeting them loudly / Feeding animals with leftover food / Taking pictures only in areas where it is allowed / Digging up clams and gathering seaweed / Not litter

Let's Review the Story

❶ Title: Sandy, the California Sea Otter

❷ Main idea

California sea otters live in a kelp forest in Monterey Bay. It is a marine protected area.

❸ Sequence

1. Sandy swims with her otter friends.
2. Sandy's mother fluffs Sandy's fur and fills it with warm, dry air.
3. Sandy is far out in the ocean. A shark follows her.
4. Sandy sees a fishing boat and swims back to the kelp forest.
5. Sandy swims around a yellow rubber boat with her brown shoe on her head.

❹ Details:

Sea otters
- live in the kelp forest in the ocean.
- have fur, webbed feet, and sharp teeth.
- sleep in a raft.
- eat snails.
- use rocks as tools.

Smart Readers: **Wise** & **Wide**

After-reading Test

- Sandy, the California Sea otter
- Level 3
- 28 Questions

(Vocabulary 7 / Reading Comprehension 16 /

Sentence Structure & Grammar 5)

1. What is the holdfast of the kelp forest?
   ① the top level
   ② the big, green fronds
   ③ the bottom of the kelp that attaches to the seafloor
   ④ the surface of the ocean

2. What is the name of the top of the kelp forest at the surface of the water?
   ① the holdfast
   ② the mid-level
   ③ the tree tops
   ④ the canopy

3. Which word is NOT related to the same body part?
   ① foot   ② kick
   ③ shoes   ④ chest

4. Which word is most similar to "sway" in meaning?

   The waves of the ocean make the kelp sway in the water.

   ① whistle   ② stop
   ③ move   ④ shine

5. Which is NOT a pair of words that are opposites?
   ① full ↔ hungry
   ② safe ↔ endangered
   ③ up ↔ down
   ④ nearby ↔ by

※ Unscramble the letters inside each box to find the answer. And write the right
answer to each question. (6~7)

6. What are all the people in the yellow rubber boat wearing?
   → ⬚ tahs ⬚   (   )

7. What special thing do the people have to look at the sea otters?
   → ⬚ lsasegs ⬚   (   )

8. Who is Sandy?
   ① a young girl
   ② a young dog
   ③ a California sea otter pup
   ④ a person who takes care of sea otters

9. What is NOT the reason Sandy closes her nostrils?
   ① She doesn't like the smell of the ocean.
   ② She wants to keep the water out.
   ③ She needs to hold her breath.
   ④ Doing that helps her dive.

10. What does ocean kelp look like?
    ① Ocean kelp is purple and looks like a starfish.
    ② Ocean kelp is green and looks like a tree in the wind.
    ③ Ocean kelp is white and looks like a house.
    ④ Ocean kelp is blue and looks like the sky.

11. Choose all the foods that Sandy and her mother eat.
    ① snails   ② starfish
    ③ kelp crabs   ④ rockfish

12. What do sea otters NOT do to make a raft while they sleep?

    ① lie in the kelp forest

    ② hold paws

    ③ float on their backs

    ④ rub their faces

13. What does Sandy's mother do to call Sandy?

    ① scream   ② whistle

    ③ sing   ④ growl

14. What makes the sound Sandy hears?

> Sandy hears the sound "thrum, thrum, thrum."

    ① the motor on a fishing boat

    ② a big shark

    ③ whistle from Sandy's mother

    ④ wind through the kelp forest

※ Choose the right word(s) to complete the answer to each question. (15~17)

15.
> How does Sandy try to open the mussel at first?
> ➜ At first, she tries to open the mussel with ___________.

    ① her mouth   ② her claws

    ③ the rock   ④ her head

16.
> How does Sandy clean the food off her thick fur?
> ➜ Sandy cleans the food off her thick fur by ___________ in the water.

    ① spinning   ② sleeping

    ③ eating   ④ breathing

17.

> What does Sandy use for her bed?
> → Sandy uses ___________ for her bed.

① a brown shoe
② rocks
③ clams
④ kelp fronds

※ Choose the right word(s) for each blank. (18~23)

18.

> Sandy's ___________ keeps her warm.

① fur   ② webbed feet
③ nostrils   ④ friend

19.

> Sandy's mother shows Sandy to hit the mussel on ___________.

① a stick   ② her head
③ her front paw   ④ a rock

20.

> Sandy is all alone. She starts to swim back to the kelp forest.
> Sandy swims almost ___________ kilometers an hour.

① nine   ② twenty
③ one   ④ fifteen

21.

> The fisherman on the boat is pulling ___________.

① sea urchins
② a fish
③ a net
④ another boat

22.

Sandy feels the water move under her. She feels something move past her very fast. The big shadow Sandy sees below her in the ocean is a ____________.

① kelp frond
② shark
③ dolphin
④ rockfish

23.

When the woman sees Sandy swim around the boat, she says Sandy is ____________.

① fast   ② cute
③ funny   ④ ugly

24. Choose the correct sentence.
   ① How some are sea snails?
   ② How about some sea snails?
   ③ How of some sea snails?
   ④ How does some sea snails?

※ Choose the right word or phrase for each blank to complete each sentence correctly. (25~28)

25.

She ____________ this far out before.

① have ever been
② has never been
③ has never be
④ have never be

26.

She swims over to take a _____________ look.

① closing   ② closes

③ closer   ④ closest

27.

It _____________.

① looks pretty

② sees pretty

③ look pretty

④ see pretty

28.

Sandy hears her mother _____________ her.

① call   ② called

③ calls   ④ to call

Suzanne Pitner
Suzanne Pitner is a teacher and writer who has enjoyed visiting Alaska, exploring Rome, teaching in China, and is looking forward to more world travel. She has a Master's Degree in Education, and is a graduate of the Long Ridge Writer's Group. In addition to writing educational articles and books, she writes historical fiction and contemporary fiction for young adults using the pen name Suzanne Lilly.

Sandy, the California Sea Otter

Written by Suzanne Pitner
Illustrated by Inlae Cho

First published December 2014
Second printing April 2022

Publisher: Kyudo Chung
Editors: Juyon Choi, Juyon Choi, Kyunghee Jang, Jiyeong Park
Designers: Eunhee Lee, Elim

Published and distributed by
Happy House, an Imprint of DARAKWON, Inc.
Darakwon Bldg., 211 Munbal-ro, Paju-si, Gyeonggi-do, 10881, Republic of Korea
Tel: 82-2-736-2031(ext. 250)   Fax: 82-2-732-2037
Homepage: www.ihappyhouse.co.kr

ISBN: 978-89-6653-162-2 18740 / 978-89-6653-156-1 18740(set)

[Components]
• 1 Audio CD (Recording Studio: Aram)
• Answer Keys & Korean Translation: Free download at www.ihappyhouse.co.kr